Cher Doll & Her Celebrity Friends

With Fashions by Bob Mackie

Sandra "Johnsie" Bryan

Also featuring the Mego® celebrity dolls for Sonny™ Bono, Farrah™ Fawcett, Diana Ross™, The Captain and Tennille™, Jaclyn Smith™, Suzanne Somers™, Wonder Woman™ and Laverne and Shirley™.

Schiffer Publishing Ltd®

4880 Lower Valley Road, Atglen, PA 19310 USA

Dedication

This book is dedicated to my granddaughters, Shannon McDaniel and Brantley Bryan. I hope they will grow to love dolls as much as I do.

Copyright © 2004 by Sandra J. Bryan
Library of Congress Control Number: 2003113320

Cover and Book Designed by Bruce Waters
Type set in Impress BT/Korinna BT

ISBN: 0-7643-1970-1
Printed in China
1 2 3 4

Published by Schiffer Publishing Ltd.
4880 Lower Valley Road
Atglen, PA 19310
Phone: (610) 593-1777; Fax: (610) 593-2002
E-mail: Info@schifferbooks.com
Please visit our web site catalog at www.schifferbooks.com
We are always looking for people to write books on new and related subjects.
If you have an idea for a book, please contact us at the above address.

This book may be purchased from the publisher.
Include $3.95 for shipping.
Please try your bookstore first.
You may write for a free catalog.

In Europe, Schiffer books are distributed by
Bushwood Books
6 Marksbury Avenue
Kew Gardens
Surrey TW9 4JF England
Phone: 44 (0) 20 8392 8585
Fax: 44 (0) 20 8392 9876
E-mail: info@bushwoodbooks.co.uk
Free postage in the UK. Europe: air mail at cost.

Disclaimer

The doll scenes in this book were created solely by the author. The dolls and products photographed for this book are from the collection of the author of this book or various private collectors. This book is not sponsored, endorsed, or otherwise affiliated with any of the companies whose products are represented here. Most of the items and products in this book may be covered by various copyrights, trademarks, and logotypes. Every effort has been made to identify these products. Their use herein is for identification purposes only. All rights are reserved by their respective owners. This book is derived from the author's independent research and creativity. All photography for this book was done by the author, who holds copyright to them. No part of this book may be reproduced without written consent of the author or publisher. Please contact Schiffer Publishing for this release.

Acknowledgments

I would like to thank two very special collectors, Linda J. Duffy-Celender and Carmen Varricchio; we began *chering* dolls and outfit finds in 1995 and built our knowledge together to the point where this book became my dream.

I am grateful for Nancy Countryman's friendship and encouragement.

Other collectors I thank for their help are Margaret Christiansen, Sue Jones McPhee, and Stan Clark of Yesterday's Heroes.

I have two terrific editors at Schiffer Publishing, Tina Skinner and Ginny Parfitt. There advice and patience made this Cher™ Doll book possible.

I *cherish* my husband John Bryan whose help and support made this book complete. I'm so glad *I Got You, Babe*!

I look forward to contacting other Cher™ doll collectors; please email me: sjbryan@austin.rr.com

Contents

Introduction - The Designer and the Corporation

What a Fabulous Designer!

Bob Mackie has become the king of costumes for Hollywood stars. After working for legendary designers Jean Louis and Edith Head, he struck costuming gold in the late 1960s with his flamboyant fashions for Mitzi Gaynor's nightclub acts and then designed the weekly *Carol Burnett Show* for eleven years. But it was for *The Sonny and Cher Comedy Hour* on CBS in the early 1970s where he established her trademark over-the-top and cut-to-there glamour gowns. For Cher, he reinterpreted 1930s vamp: she's a hippie gone to glitz!

Bob Mackie and Cher, CBS® TV photo, mid 1970s. From author's collection. Note it is autographed: "To Sandra/ love/ Bob Mackie/ 1991."

What a Coup for the Mego Corp.!

The Mego Corp. was known for manufacturing action hero toys and some dolls such as Maddie Mod™. In the mid 1970s, they contracted to produce a Cher™ doll and to copy her real Bob Mackie designs in doll-size. This was a first!

What a Doll!

The Cher™ doll is 12.25" tall, almost 1" taller than the Barbie® doll by Mattel Inc., the reigning queen of fashion dolls since 1959. The size difference makes the Cher™ doll distinct, and the clothes cannot be *chered*. Her face has a chiseled look, more realistic than that of other fashion dolls who have a "sweet and innocent" look. Her wrists rotate, her waist swivels; elbows and knees bend for a fully posable attitude. The Sonny™ doll was created as well, and he bears a strong resemblance to the star.

What a Wardrobe!

The real Cher wore Bob Mackie designs for her TV show as well as for galas and other public appearances. These were the fashions that Mego Corp. recreated, perfect little miniatures captured in doll-size. No wonder these creations were prized by fashion doll collectors from the moment they premiered in toy stores. Today they reflect the peasant tops and bell bottoms, the headbands and boots, the polyester everything from the 1970s. They are fashion history to Cher fans and doll collectors alike.

What a Nasty Trick!

The *Fickle Finger of Fate* intervened to give these dolls and their wonderful clothes a very short life. The Mego Corp. already had this line in production when the real Sonny and Cher divorced in 1975. The Sonny™ and Cher™ dolls and fashions appeared on toy store shelves in 1976 to limited enthusiasm.

What a Rally!

In 1977, Mego Corp. tried to recoup; they came out with more new celebrity dolls who could wear the Cher™ doll fashions: Farrah™ Fawcett, Diana Ross™, Toni Tennille™, Jaclyn Smith™, and Wonder Woman™. The Suzanne Somers™ doll of 1978 was the last of the Cher™ doll size to be released.

What a Find!

Mego Corp. repackaged the Cher™ doll outfits in 1981 for the Jordache® doll whose markings claimed they "fit(s) most 11.5" fashion dolls" although the clothes, and especially the shoes, were much too big. The outfits retailed for $1.98. Next, they were repackaged for the new toy store chain Toys R Us. Named "Onstage Fashions" and "In the Limelight," again they claimed to fit 11.5" dolls. Collectors knew they were Cher clothes and snapped them up, usually at bargain prices. Sadly, Mego Corp. filed for bankruptcy in 1982.

The many faces of the Mego 12.25" fashion dolls, 1976 to 1979. *Upper left to right:* Farrah™, Toni Tennille™, Diana Ross™, original Cher™ with long hair, Growing Hair Cher®, Jaclyn Smith™, Suzanne Somers™.

The Cher™ doll and her wonderful fashions by Bob Mackie had a brief but exciting shelf life. Cher fans will be amazed that they recognize most of them! This vast array of designs showcases Mackie's flair for the dramatic, his gift of the glitz, and his love for the show-biz statement. He says his talent is for creating fashions that reflect, rather than create, the star who is wearing them. It is no surprise to fashion buffs that they have endured—kind of like the real star herself! To own one of these Bob Mackie creations for Cher but in miniature is pure pleasure. Even today, Cher™ doll collectors are finding more of her fashions in the most unusual places. *And The Beat Goes On!*

Bob Mackie, promotion photo for his perfume *Mackie*. From author's collection. Note it is autographed: "To Sandra/ Bob/ Mackie/ 1991."

Chapter One
The Dolls

The Sonny™ and Cher™ dolls both premiered in 1976. There are three versions of the Cher™ doll. The Original doll has long, straight hair and sold for $7.95. In a separate package is the Sonny™ doll, and he also sold for $7.95. The Growing Hair doll has a pageboy style with bangs and a lock of hair that pulls from the crown. This doll sold for $8.95. The third doll has the Cher™ doll head placed on a less expensive hollow body and sold for $3.95.

The Sonny™ and Cher™ dolls came individually in bright orange boxes marked ©1976 Mego Corp. Manufactured Exclusively For Mego Corp. New York, N.Y. 10010 in the British Colony of Hong Kong.

The Sonny™ (Bono) doll stands 12.25" and wears a white and black poly knit shirt, denim cotton pants with two tiny gold buttons at the right waistband, and black plastic "alligator" shoes. The clothing snaps in back. $70. Mint in box.

Sonny's neck says © Mego Corp. 1976 and his rear is marked © Mego Corp 1976/ Made in Hong Kong. His neck, waist, and wrists turn, and he has bendable elbows and knees. He has a white stand, Cher™ logo underneath, and clothing brochure. The box back pictures his six outfits.

The Growing Hair Cher® doll (US and Foreign Patents Pending) comes in a hot pink box marked © 1976 Mego Corp. Manufactured by Mego Corp. New York, N.Y. 10010, in Hong Kong. Her head is marked Mego Corp./ 19©76 and her rear says © Mego Corp. 1975/ Made in Hong Kong. Her black hair is styled in a shoulder length pageboy with bangs. She has dark brown eyes and very long lashes and long nails. She wears a black and silver metallic halter dress and white open toed heels. She has a clear stand with the Cher™ logo and a clothing brochure. $75. Mint in box.

The Original Cher™ doll stands 12.25" and wears a hot pink poly halter dress which snaps in back and has open toed heels to match. Her black hair is straight, parted in the center, and reaches to mid-thighs. She has dark brown eyes with very long lashes and long sculpted nails. Her head is marked Mego Corp./ 19©75, and her rear says © Mego Corp. 1975/ Made in Hong Kong. Her head, waist, and wrists are posable, and her elbows and knees bend. She has a white stand, Cher™ logo underneath, and clothing brochure. The box back pictures seven outfits from her clothing brochure. $90. Mint in box.

Growing Hair Cher® has a hole in her back for a metal key (see upper left of box). The key winds a large lock of her hair up and down from her crown so that it appears to "grow".

Several different types of plastics were used to manufacture these dolls. The torsos appear to be melting at the arm and leg joints, but it is actually the result of a chemical reaction called out-gassing. Many dolls have blue marks on the arms, legs, or ankles as well. These are caused by a reaction between the metal wire in the limb and its surrounding plastic. Some believe these "melting" and "bruised" dolls were kept in hot attics, but the problem is chemical and not one of neglect. The dolls should be kept in air conditioning from now on to help preserve them, but it will not reverse this process.

The red box back has photos of six outfits; three are found in the clothing brochure, two are not, and one looks like a white version of an outfit actually produced in pink and green.

A third type of Cher™ doll is packaged in a red box marked ©1976 Mego Corp. and Manufactured for Mego Corp. New York, N.Y. 10010 in Hong Kong. She stands 12" with back of head markings of Mego Corp./ 19©75, and has the same head, hair, eyes and lashes as the Original Cher™ doll. This body is a less expensive hollow plastic with only a swivel waist, jointed arms and legs. Some say Hong Kong on the upper back, and some do not. She wears a stretch poly swimsuit in either yellow, red, or blue. $30-$60. Mint in box.

In the early 1980s, regular Cher™ dolls were also packaged in this box and sold for clearance prices. The hollow body Cher™ dolls were then bagged in cellophane and sold in discount stores.

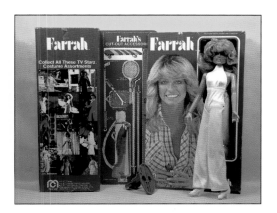

Farrah™ doll has at least two shades of hair. *Left:* more of a silver blonde; *right:* a honey blonde. Both have striking green eyes and very long lashes and nails.

Other dolls made by Mego Corp. who are the same size as the Cher™ doll include Farrah™, Toni Tennille™, and Diana Ross™. These three had small wardrobes of their own. There is a Captain™ doll to go with Tennille™. These sold for $7.95 to $8.95.

The Farrah™ (Fawcett) doll comes in a bright green box marked ©1977 Farrah Fawcett-Majors/ Manufactured Exclusively by Mego Corp., New York, N.Y. 10010, in Hong Kong. She is 12.25" and wears a white poly knit halter top jumpsuit. She has white open toed heels and a green stand, Cher™ logo underneath. There are two sizes to the boxes: one is 1" wider, but the graphics are the same. Her head back is marked Farrah, and her rear says © Mego Corp 1975/ Made in Hong Kong. $55. Mint in box.

The back of the box features the three dolls in the TV Starz™ series wearing all twelve of their outfits, four made for each doll. It also pictures sports accessories: golf bag and club, tennis racket and bag, skateboard, skis and poles.

The Toni Tennille™ doll has a red box with photo of the Captain and Tennille and is marked © 1977 Moonlight and Magnolias Inc. and Manufactured Exclusively by Mego Corp. New York, N.Y. 10010 in Hong Kong. She stands 12.25", has light brown hair in a shag hairstyle, brown eyes, and long lashes and nails. She wears a red poly dress with white sailor collar and blue ribbon bow at V neckline that snaps in back. She has white open toed heels and a white stand, Cher™ logo underneath. Her head back says ©Moonlight &/ Magnolias Inc. Her rear markings are the same as the Cher™ doll: © Mego Corp. 1977/ Made in Hong Kong. Rare, $60. Mint in box.

Daryl Dragon is the same height. He comes in an identical box (not pictured) with his name across the bottom. He wears a navy blue cotton jacket with four gold buttons and red stitching, red turtle neck poly dickey, and white cotton twill pants, a white twill captain's hat, black plastic sunglasses, and white plastic "tie" shoes. His head markings are the same as Toni Tennille, but his shoulder back says © Mego Corp 1977/ Made in Hong Kong. Rare, $60. Mint in box.

13

The Captain and Tennille box backs picture the twelve TV Starz™ fashions and their pet Bull Dogs Broderick and Elizabeth.

The Diana Ross™ doll comes in a teal blue box marked © 1977 Motown Records Corporation and Manufactured Exclusively by Mego Corp. New York, N.Y. 10010, in Hong Kong. She is 12.25" tall. The back of her head is marked © Motown Record/ Corporation and her rear says © Mego Corp 1975/ Made in Hong Kong. She has wavy black hair to her mid-back, black eyes with purple eyeshadow, long eyelashes and nails, and wears a silver metallic halter gown that snaps in back. She comes with gray open toed heels and a blue stand, Cher™ logo underneath. Rare, $125. Mint in box.

The box back features the twelve TV Starz™ outfits and a director's chair bearing her name, a camera, and microphone.

More dolls the same size as Cher™ include Jaclyn Smith™ from 1977 and Suzanne Somers™ from 1978, which sold for $7.95. These do not have their own wardrobes.

The Jaclyn Smith™ doll is 12.25" and comes in a white box marked ©1977 Mego Corp. and Manufactured Exclusively by Mego Corp. New York, N.Y. 10010 in Hong Kong. She has wavy brown hair coming past her shoulders, blue eyes, long nails, and shorter brown lashes. She wears a powder blue poly swimsuit with halter top that ties around her neck and a sheer blue tie skirt with ruffle around the edge. She comes with white open toed heels and a white stand, Cher™ logo underneath. Her head back is marked © Mego Corp and her rear has the same markings as the Cher™ doll: © Mego Corp 1975/Made in Hong Kong. Rare, $80. Mint in box.

The box back has pictures of the twelve TV Starz™ fashions and her beach hat, sandals, towel, glasses, ice cream cone, and surfboard cut-out accessories.

The Suzanne Somers™ doll stands 12.25" and has wavy light blonde hair to her shoulders, blue eyes, black lashes, and long nails. Her head back is marked © Three's/ Company and her rear says © Mego Corp 1975/ Made in Hong Kong. She wears the original Cher™ doll's hot pink halter dress and has white open toed heels and a white stand, Cher™ logo underneath. Rare, $50. Mint in box.

Her purple box says Chrissy of Three's Company/ Suzanne Somers/© 1978 Three's Company/© Mego Corp and Manufactured Exclusively by Mego Corp. New York, N.Y. 10010, in Hong Kong.

The box back pictures all three stars of *Three's Company* plus her director's chair.

The Wonder Woman™ doll has the same body as the Cher™ doll, but the head is smaller. She can wear Cher™ doll clothes and was sold for $7.95.

The Wonder Woman™ doll comes in a bright blue box with red and yellow drawings. It says Lynda Carter as Wonder Woman, ©1976 D.C. Comics Inc., and Manufactured by Mego Corp. New York, N.Y. 10010 in Hong Kong. The doll has dark brown shoulder length hair in a flip. Her head back is marked D.C. Comics/ Inc. 1976 and her rear says ©Mego Corp. 1975/ Made in Hong Kong. Rare, $250-$400.

The body of the doll has a red and yellow painted suit, stretch poly pants blue with stars, a rubbery yellow half-crown with red star, plastic silver bracelets, red boots, a gold cord lasso, and powder blue stand.

There is a second issue of this doll with the Cher doll body and a super hero action suit instead of the painted bodysuit (not pictured).

Most dolls also came with her "alter ego" outfit for Diana Prince, a navy blue cotton suit jacket and white sleeveless cotton dress with navy ribbon at neck and cotton navy skirt on a clear plastic bodyform, black open toed heels and sunglasses (now often found "melted").

Wonder Woman™ doll's body is the same as Cher™ doll's, but her head is smaller. She has very long lashes and very thick hair for her head size.

Other dolls in this series are pictured on the box back: Nubia™, Queen Hippolyte™, and Steve Trevor™, $100 each. Some box backs feature photos of outfits for Wonder Woman™.

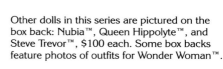

17

In 1978, the Laverne and Shirley™ dolls were produced. They have 11.5" bodies and cannot wear Cher™ doll clothes, but they have finely chiseled features like those found in this Cher™ doll series. They sold for $12.95.

Their box back has photos from their TV series. Lenny™ and Squiggy™ dolls were also available (not pictured).

The Laverne™ and Shirley™ dolls, ©1977 Paramount Pictures Corporation and Manufactured for Mego Corp., New York, N.Y. 10010 in Hong Kong, are shorter than the Cher™ doll and have bodies the size of the Barbie® doll by Mattel. They do have the same finely featured heads as the Cher™ and TV Starz™ doll series, only smaller and in proportion to their bodies. $70. Mint in box.

The Cher™ doll with her TV Starz™ friends. From left: Original Cher™, Growing Hair Cher®, Farrah™, Diana Ross™, Toni Tennille™, Jaclyn Smith™, Suzanne Somers™.

The newest Cher™ doll premiered in 2002 with the Barbie® doll body.

Bob Mackie has been creating a spectacular Barbie® Doll series for Mattel Inc. since 1990. In 2002, the company released its first Cher™ doll designed by Mackie. The box is marked © 2001 Timeless Treasures, a Collectible/Specialty Doll Division of Mattel, Inc., El Segundo, Ca. 90245 U.S.A. Made in Indonesia. This Cher™ doll is 11.5" tall and bears a striking resemblance to the celebrity. She wears a long silver metallic dress with body-baring cut-outs and a lavender boa. $85. Mint in box.

The Cher™ doll has her own dressing room, which originally sold for $7.98, as well as a theatre which sold for $19.98. A plain black vinyl doll trunk with two folding doors was sold for $5.95 (see photo with Dramatic Drizzle fashion). In 1977, Farrah™ doll had Cher™ doll's identical, but repackaged, dressing room (not shown).

Sonny and Cher's Theatre in the Round™ ©1977 by Mego Corp. is very hard to find. It is a 26" round hard plastic stage divided into three parts. There are five scenes on changeable backboards. *Left:* the Sonny and Cher TV show logo in lights; *right:* Sonny's Pizza Joint. $200 with box.

The inside has brown plastic furniture pieces: bed and pillow back, stool, and dressing table (looks like a fireplace mantle!). It features a clear plastic archway called the "magic mirror" and an attached black stand for the doll's legs. Four double-sided cards with drawings of Bob Mackie fashions can be placed in the back of this "mirror", which then reflects on the doll as if she is wearing them...much easier than trying on clothes! A black poly stretch unitard also comes with this case. $75 with box.

Cher's Dressing Room™ is by Mego Corp. ©1976. The case has two sides that open in the middle with a vinyl southwestern turquoise and brown design on the outside. The tops and bottom are turquoise hard plastic.

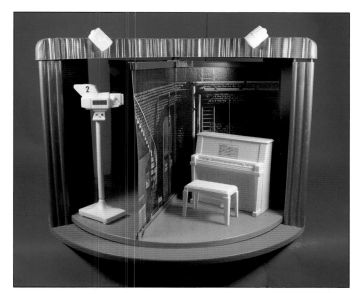

Backstage backboards. The set includes white plastic camera, piano, bench, two spotlights, and microphone (not pictured).

Dressing room backboards have a white plastic table and bench. A fifth scene, not pictured, is Onstage – a view of an audience (see photo for Radiant fashion).

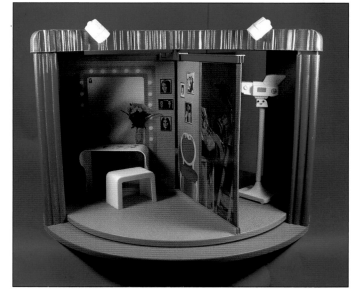

Chapter Two
Blue Blister Pak Fashions Designed by Bob Mackie

There are thirteen Blue Blister Pak fashions which were sewn to green cards. Eight are pictured in the fashion clothing brochure included with the Sonny™ and Cher™ dolls. Five more are included in 1977 Mego Corp. catalogs. These retailed for $2.98.

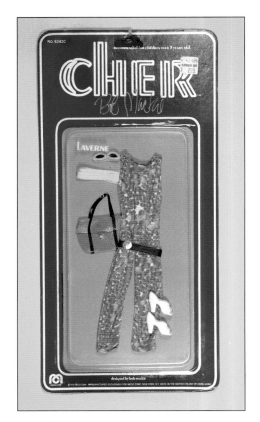

The blue blister pak fashions for Cher™, ©1976. The outfits and shoes are sewn to a green cardboard. Note this fashion, owned by the author, is signed by Bob Mackie.

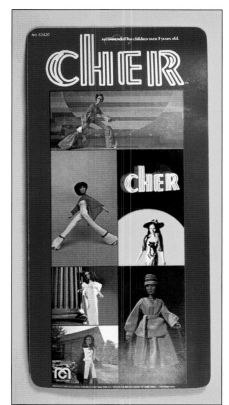

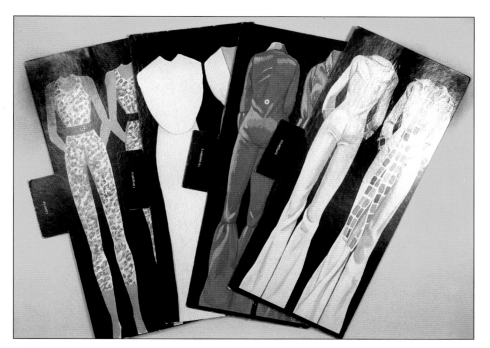

Four of the blue blister pak fashions drawn by Bob Mackie which come on cardboards in Cher's Dressing Room™: (from left) Laverne, Cleopatra, Strawberry, Jumperoo.

The blue pak back pictures six fashions in this series.

The reverse of the four cardboards with these fashions drawn by Bob Mackie: (from left) Hoedown, Chocolate Mocha, Means Business, Good Earth.

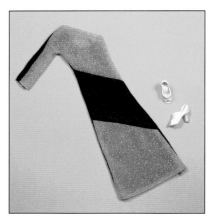

Blue Streak – gold metallic stretch fabric one sleeve gown, blue metallic wide diagonal stripe on front skirt, white heels, Rare, $60.

Back is solid blue metallic stretch fabric

"Does anybody know which track the BLUE STREAK leaves from?"

Southern Pacific train by Marx, c. 1952.
Accessories from author's collection.

Cleopatra – powder blue pleated nylon gown tied with bow, nylon panties, white heels, $25.

Back structure shows cape collar is one piece with bodice

"Hail, Caesar! Your CLEOPATRA has arrived in Rome!"

Soldier, horse, and chariot by KidKore ©1996. Headdress
©1993 by Timeless Creations/Mattel, Inc.. Background
portfolio from author's collection.

27

Good Earth – poly knit strapless gown and hat of black, white, gray and gold print, black ribbon with black felt flower and yellow rhinestone center trim, white heels, $25. *Outfit from collection of Nancy Countryman.*

Green print variation priced higher. *Photo and outfit from collection of Linda J. Duffy-Celender.*

"I have no GOOD EARTHly idea where Sonny is! He was supposed to pick me up an hour ago!"

Background from Barbie® Fashion Shop ©1962 Mattel Inc. Plants, bench, shopping bags, and watch from author's collection.

"Rub your legs together, GRASSHOPPER, and we'll make beautiful music together!"

Accessories from author's collection.

Grasshopper – green metallic stretch fabric one shoulder gown with diagonal ruffle from armhole to hem, green flower accent with pearl center on right shoulder, white heels, Rare, $75.

Hoedown – white poly stretch jumpsuit with navy blue cotton straps, navy blue cotton legs below knees and tie shirt, white platform shoes, $20.

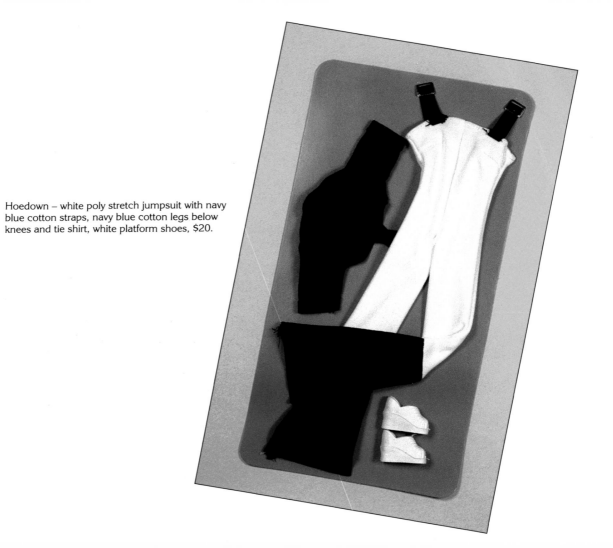

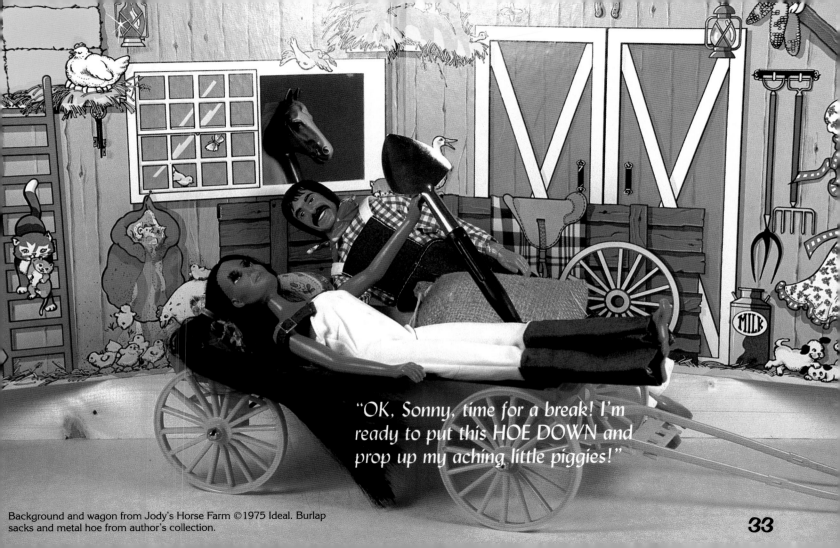

"OK, Sonny, time for a break! I'm ready to put this HOE DOWN and prop up my aching little piggies!"

Background and wagon from Jody's Horse Farm ©1975 Ideal. Burlap sacks and metal hoe from author's collection.

Image – yellow metallic stretch halter gown with black starburst design on front only, black heels. Note the photo of the 11.5" Jordache® doll by Mego and verbage on the package back. Rare, $75.

Many Cher fashions by Bob Mackie were repackaged as Jordache® Fashions ©1981 Mego Corp. Even though the package states it will fit most 11.5" dolls, it is too big. Note the Cher™ doll shoes and green cardboard backing.

"IMAGE is everything for a Hollywood Star; there is no such thing as natural beauty!"

Accessories from author's collection.

35

"We are learning the JUMPEROO and the Karate Lunge from The King himself!"

From left: Suzanne Somers™ doll in Motgomery Ward exclusive jumpsuit ©1976 Mego Corp.; Elvis™ doll ©2000 Timeless Treasure/Mattel Inc.; Cher™ doll. Backboard from Sonny and Cher's Theatre in the Round™.

Jumperoo – light green poly knit jumpsuit with multi-color check cuffs and matching scarf (unlined), zips up front, white platform shoes, $25.

Laverne – brown leopard print poly jumpsuit, dark brown vinyl belt with clear sequin buckle, light brown tote with darker vinyl handles and pearl closure, yellow ribbon, yellow plastic sunglasses with green lenses, white heels, $20.

"If you're a classic like LAVERNE, you'll never go out of style!"

1957 Chevy for Barbie® doll ©1989 Mattel Inc.

Wonder Woman™ doll ©1976 Mego Inc. Reservations Office ©1978 Sears. Bionic Woman™ Classroom bookcase (left) ©1977 Kenner. Accessories from author's collection.

Evil Doers Beware—This Woman
MEANS BUSINESS!

Means Business – blue two piece poly knit long sleeve blouse and skirt, blue and white stripe scarf with two golden metal rings, white knee high boots, $50.

Mint Julep – mint green jumpsuit with metallic green net trim at calves, matching metallic green net cape which goes over doll's head, green or white heels, $20. There are two variations: "Networks" (pink?) in ©1977 Sears Christmas Catalog and "Chocolate Mocha" (brown) in fashion brochure ©1976 Mego Corp. Variations would be priced higher because they are rare.

"A girl needs more than MINT JULEPs and promises, Rhett. Ask me to marry you again tomorrow."

...hett Butler™ doll from the *Gone With the Wind* series
...1988 World Dolls. Painting by Myrtle Barrett. Painting
...d chair from author's collection. Floor graphics
...1988 Mattel, Inc.

"Do I also want your phone # with my pizza?
Oh yes, with a PURPLE PASSION."

Backboard from Sonny and Cher Theatre in the Round™ Pizza Party set by Kitchen Littles ©1995 Tyco. Furniture, wine bottle, and glass from author's collection.

Purple Passion – one piece poly stretch jumpsuit with orange top and purple print pants, attached black vinyl belt with sequin buckle, white platform shoes, $25.

Quick Silver – silver metallic gown with
silver net puffed off-shoulder sleeves,
white heels, Very Rare, $275.

"I'm so lucky to own this beautiful mansion and be dancing with Prince Alex. And I owe it all to my Cher in the QUICK SILVER Mine!"

Czar Nicholas II doll ©1997 Galoob, from the Fox movie *Anastasia*. Ballroom scene from Barbie® and Ken® Little Theatre ©1964 Mattel Inc. Chandelier from author's collection.

Life is full of lemons, but I am a STRAWBERRY!

From left: Swing-A-Way ice crusher c. 1950s, lemon squeezer designed by Phillipe Stark and made by Alessi c. 2000, Juice-O-Mat orange juicer c. 1950s.

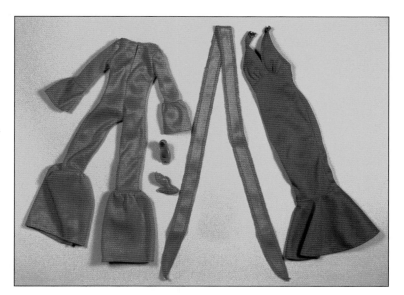

Strawberry – coral poly jumpsuit and matching scarf (hemmed but unlined), heels to match, $25. Note this fabric is lighter than the original Cher™ doll's halter dress.

"Whew! Fifty more bar presses and then I can have a little snack!"

Unitard of black stretch poly came only with Cher's Dressing Room™. Gym pieces ©1984 Mattel Inc. Cher doll outfits Starlight, original halter dress, Peek-A-Boo, and Sweets from author's collection.

Chapter Three
Green Box Cher™ Designer Collection by Bob Mackie

There are twenty Green Box fashions which were on a clear plastic bodyform sewn to a green box liner with white cotton thread. There is a drawing of the outfit on cardboard and a fashion brochure in each box. Twelve outfits are pictured in the fashion brochure, but eight more are pictured in the 1977 Mego Corp. catalogs. Each fashion sold for $5.98.

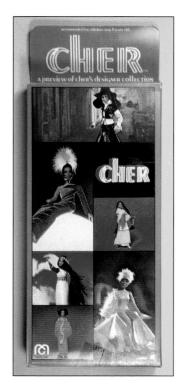

The Green Box back has photos of six outfits from the enclosed fashion brochure.

The Cher™ Designer Collection outfits come in green boxes, on a clear plastic bodyform, and then are sewn to green cardboard. The box states "designed by Bob Mackie, ©1976 Mego Corp." Each is packaged with a cardboard drawing of the outfit and a clothing brochure.

Bolero, in its green cardboard box liner.

Bolero – black vinyl split skirt and vest with nylon string ties, matching brimmed hat, white shiny poly long sleeve blouse with lace cuffs and collar, black knee boots, $50.

"When we're doing the BOLERO twirls, he doesn't always catch me!"

Background and furniture "Dinner Date" ©1985 Arco Toys

Jacket ©1965 Mattel.

53

"*I am proud to be a daughter of the CHEROKEE Nation!*"

Cherokee – tan vinyl dress with rickrack trim at waist and hem, matching rickrack headband with yarn pigtails, red/white/blue bead necklace, brown knee high boots, $50.

Another version of this dress (right) in tan poly knit with trim at high neck, waist, cuffs, and ruffled hemline.

Dragon Lady – red taffeta dress with painted yellow dragon
and red fringe at sleeves, red heels, $25.

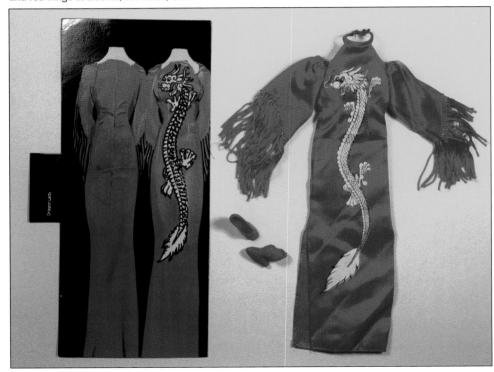

"Sailors who make a date with the DRAGON LADY are shanghaied in Astoria!"

Sonny™ doll in original outfit plus scarf. Furniture from Jody's General Store ©1975 Ideal. Parrot ©1985 Mattel Inc. "Shanghaied in Astoria" poster, © 2002 Astor Street Opry Company, Astoria, Oregon. Sailor and other accessories from author's collection.

"We're on the set for my latest movie BROCADE CA-PER. Paris is so DRAMATIC! It DRIZZLEs every evening!"

Brocade Caper cape and Dramatic Drizzle gown. Painting by Searing from author's collection. Dressing table © 1990 Mattel Inc. Camera ©Zima, no date.

Dramatic Drizzle – white and silver metallic stretch gown, silver net cape with hood (not shown), white heels. Gown only, $50; cape only, $45.

Dramatic Drizzle as pictured in the Mego Catalog ©1977 with Cher's Travel Trunk™. Trunk, $70 with box.

Dramatic Drizzle Cape is white mesh woven with silver circles and ties in the front. *Photo and cape's description courtesy of Sue Jones McPhee*

Easy Living – three pieces: poly knit powder blue blouse with gold button and cuffs, orange poly knit vest with back snap, cotton print denim pants with printed (not sewn) patchwork squares, powder blue open toed platform shoes (rare shoes), $45.

"It's EASY LIVING in the 1970s!
Just wear a Coke® and a smile!"

Hawaiian Fun Hammock ©1990 Mattel, Inc.
Other accessories from author's collection.

61

"Henny Penny and I both have ELECTRIC FEATHERS after that tornado blew through! Now we know just how Dorothy felt!"

Wizard of Oz case and accessories c. 1997 Madame Alexander Doll Co.
Card ©Pop Shots Inc., no date. Flowers and hen from author's collection.

Electric Feathers – silver metallic stretch one sleeve gown with black darts design on left side, solid silver back, matching black stretch cap with chin strap and white feather, black heels, $50. Variation: red design, priced higher.

Frosted Feathers – white one sleeve knit stretch gown with black and silver leopard spots, keyhole opening at neck, slit on left side from thigh to hem, black and white feather trim on right sleeve and slit, black or white heels. Very rare, $150.

"Frosty, my man! My FROSTED FEATHERS are falling for you!"

Snowman and sequin trees from author's collection.

"What does a GENIE wish for?
Her own Genie, of course!"

Genie – four pieces: tan and gold lace short top, balloon pants with waistband and cap, panties are solid gold knit, white platform shoes, rare, $130. This outfit also came repackaged c. 1980 in the Toys R Us® Opening Night Collection™, distributed by Lash/Tamaron Distributors, Saddlebrook, N.J. 07662, Made in Hong Kong.

The back of this green board shows how the outfit was stitched to the card, usually with one long white cotton thread, knotted at each end.

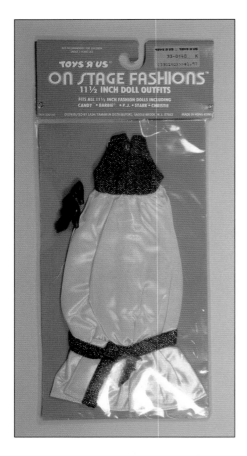

Glorious Gold – long gown with copper and black metallic top and trim on hem ruffle, gold satin skirt gathered at waist and for hem ruffle, black heels. These were repackaged c. 1980 as Toys R Us® On Stage Fashions™, Distributed by Lash/Tamaron Distributors, Saddle Brook, N.J. 07662. Made in Hong Kong. Very rare, $200.

"With this GLORIOUS GOLDen pumpkin and one wave of my magic wand, Sonny will be turned into a handsome PRINCE!"

Sonny™ doll in Space Prince fashion. Pumpkin coach from author's collection.

69

"This opera MADAME BUTTERFLY has romance, betrayal, death, and...........fashion!"

Screen and lamp from author's collection. Souvenir doll from Japan c.1960s, *gift from Betty Carroll*.

Hanky Panky –long gown with yellow and pink stretch lace top, straps, matching armlets and headband with pink feather, pink chiffon skirt with handkerchief hemline, coral heels. Very rare, $200. *Photo and outfit Mint In Box from collection of Linda J. Duffy-Celender.*

Madame Butterfly – black, red, and gold metallic woven gown with large bell sleeves, snaps around neck and in back, red heels. This dress frays easily and is difficult to find in excellent condition. Rare, $40-$75.

Madame Chan – long green brocade print coat with yellow satin cuffs and trim, matching yellow satin pants, yellow heels, $45.

The jacket came in green (most common), red, or blue and with various prints. The more unusual prints are priced higher.

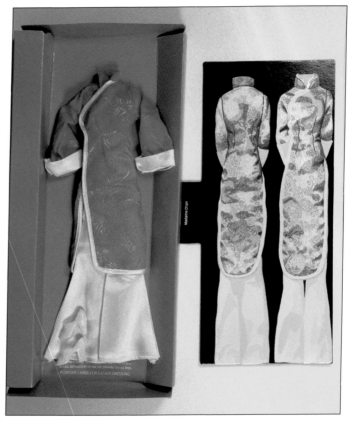

Opposite page: Capt. Li Shang doll from Disney's *Mulan* ©1997 Mattel.

MADAME CHAN *thinks rickshaw boy is plenty cute!*

Rickshaw, tree, and gong from author's collection.

"I wonder what a real PEASANT LADY fixes for dinner?"

CHECK OUT

Peasant Lady – blue stripe poly peasant top with off-shoulder sleeves, matching triangle headscarf with two gold metal rings, blue satin pants, white T-strap heels (rare), $25.

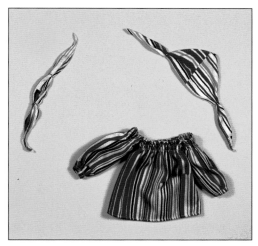

Note the same Peasant Lady fabric is used in the Means Business scarf (left) but the widths are different.

Pink Panther – deep pink stretch poly one sleeve jumpsuit, pink faux fur long sleeve, matching faux fur cap, deep pink heels, $35.

Ooh La La! PINK PANTHER,
you have my head in the
clouds!

Bendable Pink Panther™ doll ©1984 United Artists
Corp., musical metal Eiffel Tower souvenir of Paris,
c.1984 from author's collection.

77

"SPACE PRINCESS telling Astronaut how to rearrange the rock furniture."

Six Million Dollar Man ©1975 Kenner Corp.; Barbie® doll astronaut helmet and bag ©1995 Mattel Inc.; accessories from author's collection.

Space Princess – seven piece navy blue, red, silver, and gold stripe metallic stretch outfit including top with metallic silver jersey insert, two armbands, two leg cuffs, and short pants, navy blue chiffon tie cape, blue knee high boots, $35.

Sadie – dress of pink and yellow stretch lace top with attached orange satin skirt, V insert of white cotton with orange rickrack trim, matching stretch lace hat with pink and white feathers. Very rare, no price available. *Outfit and photo from collection of Stan Clark of Yesterday's Heroes*

Stepping Out – two piece outfit with green and gold stretch metallic print jumpsuit, silver and rhinestone bodice ornament, mint green skirt (front seams unhemmed) that attaches to bodice ornament with elastic thread, mint green heels, $25.

Wirehair Fox Terrier "Best of Show" series c.2002 Country Artists®; Backboard and lawn from Barbie's Surprise House™, ©1974 Mattel Inc.

"I'm STEPPING OUT with my best little sweetheart, Jackson!™"

81

"On a SUNKISSED day like today, I go topless!"

Jaguar ©1998 Mattel, Inc., purse ©1965 Mattel, Inc., tree from author's collection.

82

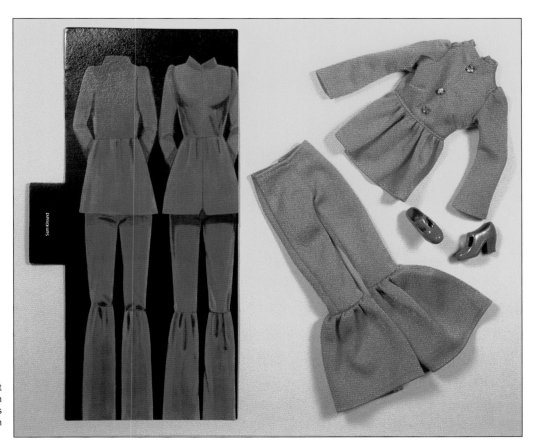

Sunkissed – deep orange iridescent poly knit two piece pantsuit with three yellow rhinestones as buttons down the center of the top, brown T-strap heels (rare), $55.

Sweater Girl – two piece outfit includes yellow poly knit top with brown velour stripe on sleeve and cuffs, matching velour split skirt, brown knee high boots, Very rare, $150.

"The SWEATER GIRL always goes to the head of the class!"

GEOGRAPHY

Dolls, *back row from left:* Blues Brothers doll "Mack" ©1997 Toy Biz, Farrah™ doll ©1977 Mego Corp.; *front row from left:* Sonny™ doll ©1996 Mego Corp., Daryl Dragon, aka The Captain™ doll ©1977 Moonlight and Magnolias Inc. and Mego Corp., Gay Bob™ doll ©1977 Harvey Rosenberg. Pink locker ©1984 Mattel Inc., schoolroom accessories ©1996 Arco/Mattel Inc.

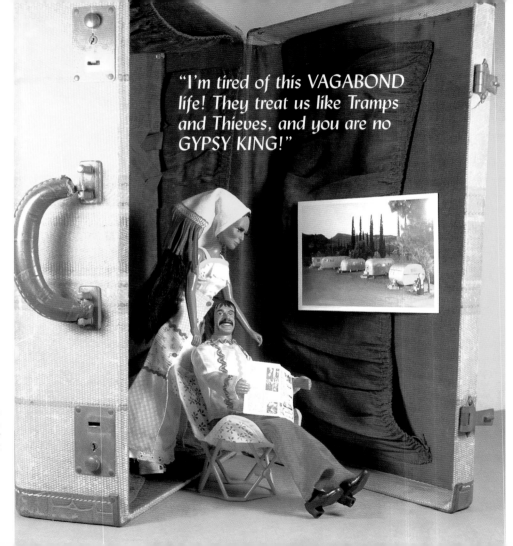

"I'm tired of this VAGABOND life! They treat us like Tramps and Thieves, and you are no GYPSY KING!"

Sonny™ doll in Gypsy King fashion. Butterfly chair c.1991 Mattel Inc., Trailer photo © 2000 Terrence Moore on stationery ©Palm Press Inc., vintage suitcase *gift from Mavis Sessions Royer.*

Vagabond – three piece outfit including a white cotton dress with eyelet lace at top and hem, yellow poly knit trim at neckline and for straps, matching yellow poly knit shawl with red nylon fringe, skirt of patched cotton in two prints: orange roses and yellow checks that attaches around waist by metal "a" hook, white T-strap heels or white platforms, $35.

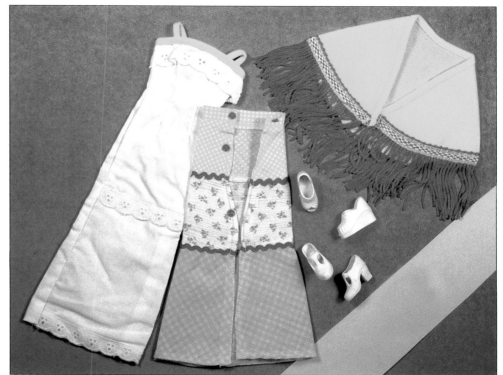

Chapter Four

Purple Box Cher™ Designer Collection by Bob Mackie

There are twelve Purple Box fashions which were on a clear plastic bodyform sewn to a purple box liner with white cotton thread. Each box includes the outfit drawn on cardboard and the fashion brochure. All of these are pictured in the fashion brochure.

The purple box fashions are marked "Cher™ Designer Collection, Designed by Bob Mackie, ©1976 Mego Corp."

Fortune Teller – a black and silver stretch metallic gown with black and silver trim, matching cap with chin strap, center bodice has metal and rhinestone ornament (like Stepping Out) backed by black felt, black heels. This fabric is more silver than Electric Feathers. $40.

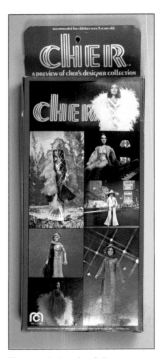

The purple box back has photos of seven fashions.

88

"You need to be a FORTUNE TELLER to win in this town!"

Left: Farrah™ doll ©1977 Mego Inc. in 1976 Montgomery Ward exclusive fashion by Mego Corp. Furniture © 1982 and ©1990 Mattel Inc. Roulette set by Ocean Desert Sales. Backboard from Stratosphere Casino, Las Vegas, NV. Gaming miniatures from author's collection.

"This FOXY LADY can outsmart a PRIVATE EYE anytime!"

90

Foxy Lady – two piece outfit includes pink metallic jumpsuit overlaid with black lace on the top. Attached is a lace skirt with black fringe around each knee. Matching black lace cape with collar lined in pink metallic fabric that ties, black heels, $60.

Gown of Paradise – deep orange stretch poly
one shoulder gown with attached scarf,
embroidered in blue and gold with peacock
design, caramel heels (rare), $50.

Travel accessories from author's collection.

"In my GOWN OF PARADISE, I can chill out and meditate just like Buddha!"

Purse ©1961 Mattel Inc., miniature paintings and accessories from author's collection.

"If he was really HALF AND HALF, how could he tell if he's coming or going?"

Half and Half – two pieces including bright pink metallic fabric short jacket trimmed with black metallic edges and cuffs, matching black metallic pants with pink metallic waistband, black heels or white platform shoes, $25. The black metallic fabric is the same as Fortune Teller.

Herky Jerky – three pieces in blue metallic fabric. Bra top and waistband have a silver and floral trim, jacket fronts are lined, white heels, $25.

"After we've learned the HERKY JERKY, Let's Hustle!"

a left: Suzanne Somers™ doll ©1978 Mego Inc. in 1976 Montgomery Ward exclusive fashion by Mego Corp. Cher™ doll *...rky Jerky fashion; Mod Hair Ken™ doll ©1973 Mattel Inc.; Ken™ doll c. 1995 Mattel Inc.; Gay Bob™ doll ©1977 Harvey ...nberg; Farrah™ doll ©1977 Mego Corp. in Let's Hustle fashion. Tinsel dance cage is 2002 Rocky Mountain Mod *...ie® Doll Convention souvenir. Furniture from Café Today ©1971 Mattel Inc. Other accessories from author's collection.*

97

"Admit it; no INDIAN SQUAW ever looked this groovy!"

Sonny™ doll in BUCKSKIN fashion. Case is Cher's Dressing Room™ ©1976 Mego Corp. Accessories from author's collection.

Indian Squaw – five piece outfit of silver metallic fabric with chevron design including a halter tie top, long split skirt, two armlets, and long yellow feather headdress, yellow platform shoes (rare), $75.

La Plume – this Mint in Box fashion is autographed by Bob Mackie!

La Plume - blue, tan, and white print metallic stretch jumpsuit with blue feathers at wrists and ankles, white heels, $30-$50.

Sonny ™ doll in TUX fashion.
Backboard, piano, and bench
from Sonny and Cher's Theatre
in the Round ™.

All decked out as LA PLUME, and sing-
ing, "She was a scamp, camp, and a bit
of a tramp, she was a V-A-M-P, vamp."

101

"Way to Go! MIDNIGHT BLUE won by a nose!"

Midnight Blue – three piece outfit with a blue metallic skirt, brimmed hat, and vest attached to a pink metallic long sleeve shirt, blue knee high boots, $30.

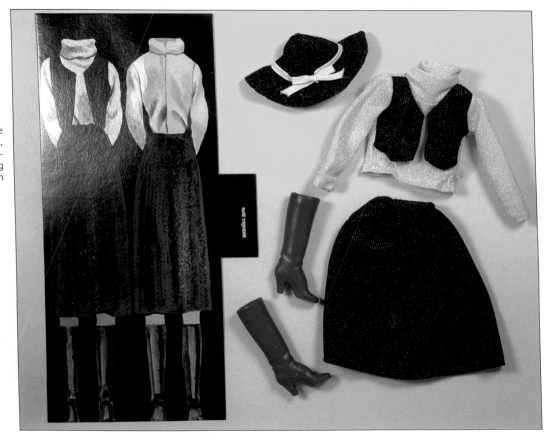

Pink Fluff – white nylon gown, long pink chiffon overcape with white feather trim, white heels, $50. (A green version of this outfit called Mint Parfait is featured in the black box line.)

"I am the famous author Shannon Brantley, but my romance novels are more than just PINK FLUFF."

Sofa ©1998 Prys-Dritz; Godiva chocolates c. 1999 Mattel, Inc. Other accessories from author's collection.

105

"*Congratulations to our winner! You have never been more RADIANT than you are tonight!*"

Left: Blues Brothers doll "Mack"™, ©1997 Toy Biz; podium from "Dinner Date" Set ©1985 Arco Toys, award ©1988 Mattel, Inc., posed in Sonny and Cher's Theatre in the Round™

Radiant – silver metallic stretch gown with red V design down front side only, white feather boa, red heels. Note that this outfit was repackaged with a faux fur boa, right. $35.

Starlight – gold and black metallic net gown over white nylon strapless gown, matching one piece hemmed cap and long scarf, ending in hood, scarf, black heels, $35. (This outfit or a variation was renamed Charisma in the 1977 Mego Corp. catalog.)

"STARLIGHT, Star bright, First star
I see tonight———I wish———."

Background Barbie® Surprise House
©1972 Mattel Inc., sofa ©1977 Mattel
Inc. Tree, gifts and accessories from
author's collection.

"We're WHITE OUT of Charlie's Angels!" (Sorry, Sabrina!)

From left: Jaclyn Smith™ doll in Toni Tennille™ doll's fashion Shop Around; Cher™ doll; Farrah™ doll in Knockabouts top and Montgomery Ward exclusive fashion pants © 1976 Mego Corp.

White Out – four piece outfit with white stretch poly knit jacket, pants, and brimmed hat, lavender sleeveless turtleneck poly knit blouse, matching lavender poly knit cuffs and hat trim, white platforms, $40. This outfit has detailed pockets and stitched front seams.

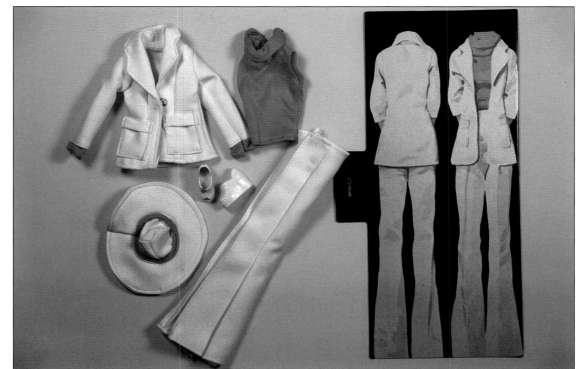

The 1977 Mego Corp. catalogs picture nine more of these purple box fashions. These have been found with green stickers stating "Fits-Font Sur Farrah" and are believed to have been sold only in Canada and Europe. These are the hardest to find and are now the most expensive to own.

CHER - 9 COSTUME ASSORTMENT
62430

Dainty Damsel
Indian Squaw
Radiant Ruffles
Peek A Boo
Let's Hustle
Rodeo Roundup
Star Brite

Tara
Charisma
Blushing Bride
Fortune Teller
Beautiful Dreamer

CHER

The Mego Corp. Catalog ©1977 features nine outfits packaged in the purple fashion boxes but with added green labels reading "Fits-Font Sur Farrah" and released for the Canadian and European markets. These are very rare and highly prized by American collectors. Pricing is over $200 in online auctions.

Upper right: Star Brite – silver metallic gown with blue starburst design, white feather boa, white heels; *2nd row center:* Blushing Bride – "long white dress, matching veil, white plastic flowers, white shoes" (from McMasters Auction Catalog description, March 1999); *2nd row right:* Rodeo Roundup – "rust colored o/f with white and brown chaps, vest and belt, white hat, brown shoes" (from same McMasters Catalog); *3rd row left:* Let's Hustle – see photo this chapter; *3rd row right:* Tara – "long green print ruffled dress with green velveteen bodice, mint green shoes" (from same McMasters Catalog), Tara also pictured in Cher's Travel Trunk™ photo – see photo for Dramatic Drizzle fashion; *4th row left:* Peek-A-Boo – see photo this chapter; *4th row center:* Dainty Damsel – see photo this chapter; *4th row right:* Beautiful Dreamer – white ruffled jumpsuit, pink and white lace overcoat, white heels; *lower right:* Radiant Ruffles – no description available, photo suggests purple long skirt or full pants and jacket with green blouse. Also pictured on this Mego Corp. Catalog page are *upper left:* Indian Squaw and *2nd row left:* Fortune Teller – from the fashion brochure series, and *lower right:* Charisma – photo suggests it is the same as Star Light.

Dainty Damsel – dress of white nylon dotted sleeves, white apron panel, black twill vest with yellow trim, red satin skirt, nylon dotted hat with red ribbon, white heels. *Photo and outfit Mint in Box from collection of Carmen Varricchio.*

Left: Let's Hustle – silver and brown stripe metallic pants and vest, peach sheer nylon blouse with tie at neck, brown T-strap heels. This outfit was found repackaged as a Toys R Us special. *Right:* Peek-A-Boo – green pleated nylon robe with bodice, cuffs, and panties of green and gold print stretch poly (same as Stepping Out jumpsuit), green heels.

Chapter Five

Black Box Cher™ Boutique Collection by Bob Mackie

There are six black box fashions that were on clear plastic bodyforms sewn to hot pink box liners. These are NOT in the fashion brochure; they are pictured in the 1977 Mego Corp. catalogs only. These were sold in department stores for $4.95; they are hard to find and highly prized by collectors.

The Black Box back has photos of five fashions. Upper right and middle right fashions were not released.

The Black Box Cher Boutique Collection ©1977 Mego Corp. Fashions designed by Bob Mackie.

Brocade Caper – silver and blue metallic cape in diamond pattern, silver metallic stretch bloomers, white knee high boots, $70. *Photo in scene for Dramatic Drizzle fashion.*

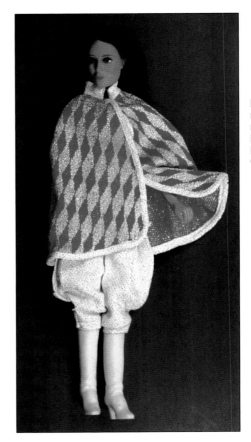

Brocade Caper has no blouse and does not include a hat, but it is shown with these in the 1977 Mego Corp. catalog.

Liberty Belle – colonial style dress with blue velour top and skirt overlays, red and white stripe cotton skirt, white satin ruffles at neckline, cuffs, and hem, red ribbon bows at cuffs and overlays, white satin nightcap with red ribbon, white heels, rare, $75.

"You can borrow my *LIBERTY BELLE*, but please don't ask me to sew the flag. How about trying Betsy?"

George Washington doll ©1997 Soldiers of the World/ K-Mart . Furnishings from author's collection.

"You can have your chocolate. My favorite flavor is MINT PARFAIT!"

Ginny™ doll Sweet Shop ©1979 Vogue Dolls, Inc. Furniture ©2002 Mattel Inc. Inc. Accessories from author's collection.

Left: Mint Parfait; *right:* Pink Fluff. The overcapes are the same chiffon with white feather trim. White nylon gown worn underneath, white heels, very rare, $125.

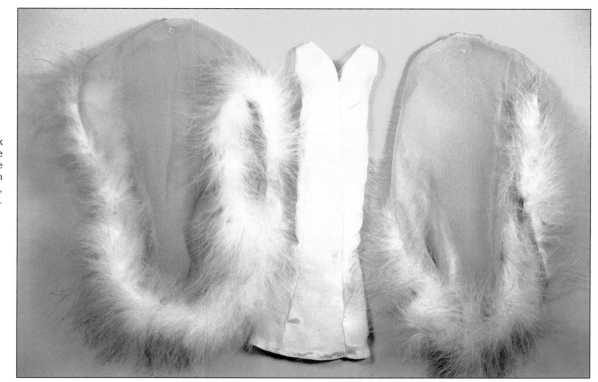

Mother Goose – long dress of green and pink metallic pieced stripes with off-shoulder sleeves and skirt, attached lace-up black velour vest, green heels. Hat is black felt circle with green and pink feathers. *Hat photocopy courtesy of Linda J. Duffy-Celender, re-colored by author*) Rare, $75.

"Look out, kiddies; this MOTHER GOOSE tells Fractured Fairy Tales!"

Soft sculpture marketed by Wal-Mart Stores Inc., no date. Other accessories from author's collection.

Painting of Tillamook Head, Oregon by Jean Barney from author's collection.

Stormy Weather – heavy vinyl black coat, brimmed hat and belt, rabbit trim on cuffs and hem, black knee high boots, very rare, $125.

Velvet Lady – long dress with pink and green print organdy peasant top, rose velour skirt with ruffle, waist trimmed with brown oilcloth and yellow velour lace-up belt accessory (attached), yellow velour trim at ruffle, rose velour shawl, yellow heels, very rare, $125. Top frays very easily.

"In the 1970s, we were not afraid to wear VELVET LADY clothes and oriental polyester prints. Everything went with everything else because we had no taste!"

Left: Cher™ doll; *right:* Jaclyn Smith™ doll in Montgomery Ward exclusive fashion by Mego Corp. Background and furniture from Barbie's Apartment™, a department store special ©1975 Mattel Inc.

Chapter Six
Other Mego®Celebrity Doll Fashions

The Sonny™ doll has six fashions. Each was in a green box, on a clear plastic bodyform, sewn to the green cardboard liner, and retailed for $5.98. The box is NOT marked as designed by Bob Mackie.

Sonny™ doll fashions came in a green box ©1976 Mego Corp.

The box back shows Sonny's six outfits.

Buckskin – three piece outfit with a black and tan fringed oil-cloth jacket, black oilcloth pants, orange stretch poly sleeveless top, black shoes, $30. (The oilcloth is now disintegrating, even Mint in Box, and many have white dots caused by chemical outgassing.) *Photo in scene for Indian Squaw fashion.*

Gypsy King – three piece outfit of white satin shirt with yellow and red rickrack, red velour pants, rickrack tie belt, black shoes, $30. *Photo in scene for Vagabond fashion.*

127

Space Prince – three piece outfit of blue metallic knit (same as Cher™ doll's Midnight Blue outfit) top, pants and belt. Silver metallic knit sleeves and neck insert. Seamed belt has silver oilcloth buckle and snaps in back, black shoes, $40. *Photo in scene for Glorious Gold fashion.*

Hoedown – three piece outfit of navy blue twill overall trimmed with white twill straps and cuffs, blue and white checkered cotton shirt, red and white polka dot cotton triangular scarf, black shoes, $30. *Photo in scene for Cher's Hoedown fashion.*

Private Eye – four pieces with tan twill overcoat and tie belt, brown cotton pants, yellow stretch ribbed poly top, black shoes, $30. *Photo in scene for Foxy Lady fashion.*

Tux – three pieces including a white woven poly jacket and pants trimmed with gold metallic knit, white satin shirt with gold metallic knit bowtie. Jacket has two gold buttons, white shoes, $40. *Photo in scene for La Plume fashion.*

Some Cher™ doll fashions were repackaged as Farrah™ fashions. The box stated "designed by Bob Mackie." These retailed for $4.49.

The Farrah™ doll has four outfits in the TV Starz™ Fashion Collection. These were in a green blister pak sewn to a green card. These were sold for $2.98. They are NOT marked as designed by Bob Mackie.

Many of Cher™ doll's fashions were repackaged as Farrah™'s Fashions ©1977 Mego Corp. The green card inside has printed instructions to powder "Cher's" legs to make it easier to put on the boots.

The Farrah™ outfits known to be produced were sold as "TV Starz Fashion Collection", ©1977 Farrah, Manufactured by Mego Corp. These are sewn to a green card inside a green blister pak.

The Farrah's™ Fashions green box has photos of eight outfits. They resemble some Cher™ outfits, but were they produced?

The back of the Farrah™ box pictures twelve outfits, four for Farrah™, four for Diana Ross™, and four for Toni Tennille™.

Left: Farrah™ doll with guitar©1996 Trend Masters Inc. *right:* Jaclyn Smith™ doll in Montgomery Ward exclusive fashion ©1976 Mego Corp. Background is Barbie® Surprise House © 1972 Mattel Inc., chair ©1983 Mattel Inc. Accessories from author's collection.

"I love to get down and play some full-tilt BOOGIE BLUES!"

Most of the TV Starz™ series were later repackaged as Jordache® fashions. Collectors could tell which doll they were designed for by the color of the cardboard inserts and the fact that the doll's name was printed on it with directions to use powder when putting on her boots.

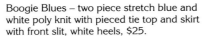

Boogie Blues – two piece stretch blue and white poly knit with pieced tie top and skirt with front slit, white heels, $25.

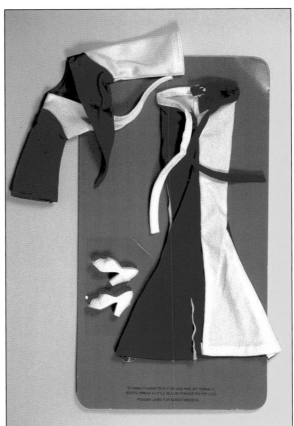

Highlights – black poly strapless gown with silver rickrack at top and hem, front only, metallic silver and black jacket (same as Fortune Teller), black heels, $25. This outfit was also sold in the J.C. Penney Christmas Catalog ©1977 and as a Jordache® fashion ©1981 Mego Corp.

"This is definitely one of the HIGH-LIGHTS of being a Hollywood Star!"

Various dolls from author's collection, "cement" drawing by author.

Horse Dancer ©1971
Mattel Inc. Background
from Barbie® and
Ken® Little Theatre
©1964 Mattel Inc.

*"Whoa, KNOCKABOUTS!
Now I know how you got
your name!"*

Knockabouts – red turtleneck poly top, red and green plaid cotton bloomer pants, red knee high boots (like Wonder Woman™ doll), $30. This outfit was also sold in the J.C. Penney Christmas catalog ©1977 and as a Jordache® fashion ©1981.

Visions – metallic pink one
sleeve gown, pink heels, $25.

Visions repackaged as a Jordache® fashion ©1981 Mego Corp.

Tool belt and hard hat ©1995
Mattel Inc., travel poster of Hoover
Dam from author's collection.

"You have to have Big
VISIONS to accomplish
Big Things!"

"Cross my palm with silver and my GYPSY MAGIC will tell your future!"

Left: Cher ™ doll in the orange Montgomery Ward exclusive fashion; *right:* Toni Tennille ™ doll in Gypsy Magic. Disney's "Hunchback of Notre Dame" Festival Tent ©1996 Arco Toys/ Mattel Inc. Accessories from author's collection.

The Toni Tennille™ doll has four outfits in a red version of the blister pak. These sold for $2.98 as well. These are NOT marked as designed by Bob Mackie.

The TV Starz™ Fashion Collection for Toni Tennille™ are in red blister paks marked Captain and Tennille™, Toni Tennille™, ©1977 Moonlight and Magnolias, Inc. Manufactured by Mego Corp.

Gypsy Magic is similar to the orange "On Stage Fashions™" made for Toys R Us, Distributed by Lash/Tamarom Distributors, Saddle Brook, N.J. 07662 c. 1980. Before that, the orange dress was a Montgomery Ward exclusive fashion ©1977 Mego Corp. (Note the rare caramel heels packaged with this outfit.)

Gypsy Magic – Dress has a pink and white nylon top, pink velour belt and white poly skirt with three different rickrack trims, white heels, $25.

The Toni Tennille™ outfits were also found repackaged as Jordache® fashions ©1981 Mego Corp.

Shop Around – two piece red poly pantsuit with red and white polka dot collar and scarf (drawn), white platform shoes, $25. *Photo in scene for White Out fashion.*

Sunshine – pink poly stretch dress with pink and white floral nylon ruffles at neck and two tiers at hem, pink heels, $25. Variation: Yellow poly.

"SUNSHINE and ocean breeze kisses! Every cruise is a honeymoon for my captain and me!"

The Captain waits for Tennille to change fashions.

bie® Dream Boat case ©1975
tel Inc. Painting by Ginger Wilson.
author's collection.

The Captain™ doll, Daryl Dragon, wears a dapper nautical three piece suit, captain's hat and sunglasses. Accessories from author's collection.

"We sing—do—be—
do—be—dee—in
SWEET HARMONY!"

From left: Diana Ross™ doll in Summer Breeze; Farrah™ doll in Montgomery Ward exclusive fashion; Toni Tennille™ doll in Sweet Harmony. Background from Sonny and Cher's Theatre in the Round™ ©1977 Mego Corp.

Sweet Harmony – long white poly sundress with sheer green nylon floral and polkadot bodice, ruffle at hem, and overcoat; white heels, $25. Pink lace variation priced higher.

The Diana Ross™ doll has four outfits as well, but in a blue version of the bubble pak (not pictured). These are NOT marked as designed by Bob Mackie.

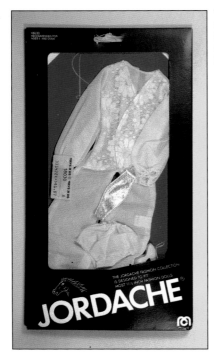

The Diana Ross™ doll outfits were packaged in a blue version of the TV Starz™ Fashion Collection (not shown). They were repackaged as Jordache® fashions ©1981 Mego Corp. Note the blue cardboard liner.

Golden Lady – yellow nylon one piece jumpsuit with attached yellow lace vest on front, yellow plastic pants, silver metallic knit belt with snap in back, yellow heels, $40.

"The GOLDEN LADY of Easter is getting help hiding the eggs from all her little bunnies!"

"MOON RIDER on the Pacific Coast Highway!"

Moon Rider – powder blue poly jumpsuit with halter top and white faux fur trim at Capri length legs, matching blue poly jacket with white faux fur trim on sleeves, three white buttons, white platform shoes, $40.

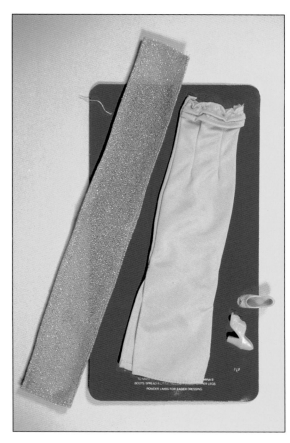

Rhymes – mint green poly strapless gown, metallic green hemmed shawl, mint green heels, $30.

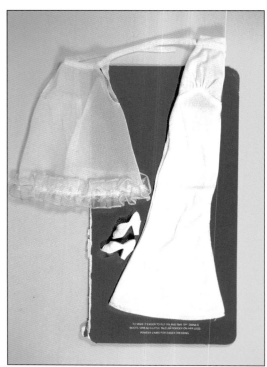

Summer Breeze – white poly gown with halter top, sheer white nylon top that ties at neck back and has ruffle at hem trimmed in pink, white heels. *Photo in scene for Sweet Harmony.*

We need a catchy name. What RHYMES with "green?" How about "Supreme?"

m left: Diana Ross™ doll in ymes; Live Action Christie™ 1 ©1971 Mattel Inc. in Peek-3oo; Cara™ doll ©1975 ttel Inc. in Stepping Out. :kground from Sonny and er's Theatre in the Round 977 Mego Corp.

Chapter Seven

Mego® Exclusive Cher Doll Fashions for Montgomery Ward

In the 1976 and 1977 Christmas Catalogs, Montgomery Ward offered thirteen outfits in groups of four "Fashions to Fit the Cher™ Crowd," which sold for $5.96. They arrived in a white cardboard box with a black and white photocopy of the outfits inside, which were individually packaged in cellophane. The first year, two groups of four designs were advertised; for the second year, there were five new outfits, two were repeated, and one came in another fabric variation. These fashions are NOT marked as designed by Bob Mackie, but several are the same pattern as earlier outfits accredited to him.

Montgomery Ward sold four exclusive fashions in a white cardboard box. *Top:* 1976 fashions; *bottom:* 1977 fashions. *Photocopy courtesy of Margaret Christiansen.*

The Montgomery Ward Christmas catalogs picture exclusive Cher™ doll fashions sold in groups of four. Top row shows groups H and J from 1976. Bottom row shows groups A and B from 1977. Two are repeated, five are new, and one is a variation from the previous year.

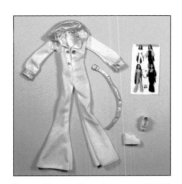

Group H – white poly jumpsuit with metallic gold jersey cuffs, collar and belt, white platform shoes, $40. *Belt from collection of Carmen Varricchio. Photo in scene for Jumperoo fashion.*

Group H – metallic blue gown with metallic pink and silver metallic batwing sleeves, black and silver rickrack trim, white heels, $30. Note the two gowns are different lengths.

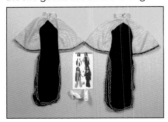

The blue batwing gown from Group H and the green variation from Group B.

Cher and Cher Alike.

Group H – pink fringe top and metallic purple pants, white heels, $35. *Photo in scene for Herky Jerky fashion.*

Group H – black metallic gown with black net sleeves and ornament of silver flower, blue rhinestone and black ribbon, black heels, $40. This was later repackaged as an "OnStage Fashions™" for Toys R Us. *Photo in scene for Fortune Teller fashion.*

Group J – one sleeve white and silver lace gown, white heels, $50. *Photo in scene for Sweet Harmony fashion.*

Group J – pink poly tie top and amoeba print metallic pants, pink shoes, $35. *Photo in scene for Boogie Blues fashion.*

Group J – red and tan chevron stripe top, tan poly pants with sewn front seam, hemmed belt with cotton fringe, white heels, $45. *Photo in scene for Peasant Lady fashion.*

Group J – red oriental poly print gown with halter top, jacket, both trimmed in gold rickrack, red heels, $40. *Photo in scene for Velvet Lady fashion.*

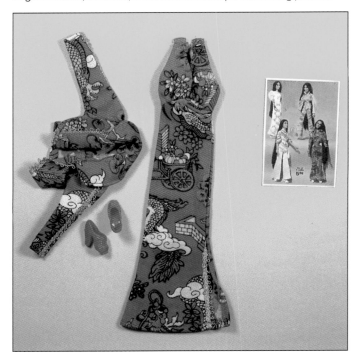

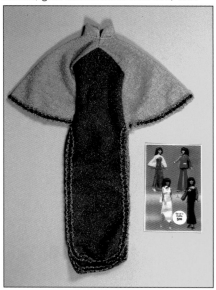

Group B – variation on the batwing gown in metallic green with tan and gold metallic sleeves, gold and black rickrack trim, $50.

Group A – orange peasant gown with net top and ruffed hem, poly skirt, brown oilcloth waist, brown ribbon and hem trim, rare brown heels, $75. *Photo in scene for Gypsy Magic fashion.*

Group B – blue poly pantsuit with red, white, and blue rickrack, white platform shoes. $45. *Photo and outfit from collection of Linda J. Duffy-Celender.*

Chapter Eight

Chering Trivia

Those Shoes!

There were three types of shoes for the Cher™ doll and her friends: open toe heels, open toe platform shoes, and closed toe T-strap heels. The heels came in white, black, mint green, red, yellow, caramel, gray, and at least three shades of pink to coral. These were the most common shoe, with white and black the most plentiful and caramel and gray the rarest colors. Platform shoes came in either powder blue (one outfit), yellow (one outfit), or white (most common). The T-straps are rare and came in caramel or white only. **Collectors should be aware that the particular shoes included with an outfit may vary, especially in those fashions that were repackaged.**

The doll also wore two types of knee-high boots: one has an even edge and came in blue (most common), black, brown, or white (rare). The red boots with a higher edge at knee side came with Wonder Woman™ doll and one Farrah™ doll fashion.

The Sonny™ doll wore a high tongue "alligator" shoe in either black or white (one outfit).

A shoe for every hour!

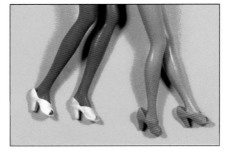

These heels were made for walking—on Cher™ doll's feet (*left*), not Barbie® doll's (*right*).

Those Clothes!

The fashion brochure *Cher™ Designer Collection* came packaged with the Sonny™ and Cher™ dolls, the green box fashions, and purple box fashions. It featured thirty-two of the outfits for Cher™, the six for Sonny™, and Cher's Dressing Room™.

This fashion brochure came with the Sonny™ and Cher™ dolls and in the green box and purple box fashions. Some of these prototypes vary from the outfits actually marketed.

That Tag!

One piece of each outfit is labeled: a paper tag is found sewn inside a seam. It reads, "Mego/Made in Hong Kong." Some of the tags are sewn inside out or upside down. It is amazing how many of these fragile tags have survived!

A paper tag sewn in one seam says "Mego®/ made in Hong Kong." Most tags also have an alphabetical letter such as A or D, probably a manufacturing record.

These Stars!

These wonderful miniature Bob Mackie fashions all began with the Cher™ doll.

The 1976-1978 Mego Corp. celebrity fashion doll lineup, *from left:* Cher™ doll, Farrah™ doll, Toni Tennille™ doll, Diana Ross™ doll, Jaclyn Smith™ doll, and Suzanne Somers™ doll.

Sonny™ doll in clothing from author's collection, Cher™ doll in Diana Ross™ doll's original outfit. Background from Sonny and Cher's Theatre in the Round™ ©1977 Mego Corp.

And The Beat Goes On!

This *Dark Lady* can sure *Turn Back Time!*

She is the doll with the "mostest." Here are my candidates:

Most Famous Outfits: Indian Squaw, La Plume.
Most Definitely From the 70s: Jumperoo, Sunkissed, Velvet Lady, White Out.
Most Vintage / Vamp: Fortune Teller.
Most Delicate: Madame Butterfly.
Most in A Category all its Own: Glorious Gold (just read the description!).
Most Likely To Be Worn to the 70s Prom: Pink Fluff, Good Earth.
Most Corny: Hoedown, Space Princess, Cherokee.
Most Fun: Laverne, Pink Panther, the Dressing Room.
Most Classic: Gown of Paradise, Madame Chan.

Most Beautiful But Strange: Foxy Lady.
Most Over-the-Top: Frosted Feathers, Hanky Panky, Mother Goose.
Most Down-to-There: Strawberry, Cleopatra, Peek-A-Boo.
Most Likely Named After Cocktails: Grasshopper, Mint Julep, Purple Passion.
Most Likely Still in your Mother's Closet: Let's Hustle, Means Business.
Most Elusive: Dramatic Drizzle, Quick Silver, the Theatre.
Most Impossible to Find: Sadie, Chocolate Mocha, the foreign outfits.
Most Really "Cher": Herky Jerky, Half and Half, Electric Feathers, Image.

Annotated Bibliography

Bryan, Sandra Johnsie. *Coffee with Barbie® Doll*. Atglen, Pennsylvania: Schiffer Publishing Ltd, 1998. *More fun scenes from the author's doll collection.*

Bono, Sonny. *And The Beat Goes On*. New York: Pocket Books, 1991. *His version, straight up but with a twist of wry.*

Carroll, Scott. "Mego Past and Present." www.megomuseum.com. Posted February 1999. Accessed 17 January 2003. *Mego Catalog pages and history.*

Mackie, Bob and Gerry Bremer. *Dressing for Glamour*. New York: A & W Publishers, 1979. *About the man and his fabulous costume designs for the stars.*

O'Connell Myers, Kristi. "Cher." www.hieroglyph.net/cher1.html Posted 25 November 2001. Accessed 17 January 2003. *Mego Catalog pages and photos from her collection.*

Pellegrino, Vicki. *Superstar of the Seventies: Cher!* New York: Ballantine Books, 1975. *An unauthorized version.*

Pence Anderson, Penny. "Bob Mackie: Designing the Cher That Meets the Eye." *TV Showpeople Magazine*. August 1975: 30+ *Photos of wonderful Mackie costumes designed for Cher.*

Varricchio, Carmen. *Collectible Doll Fashions: 1970s*. Atglen, Pennsylvania: Schiffer Publishing, Ltd. 2002. *Includes some Mint in Box Cher fashions.*

Index